SEE-ZERS

Games and Puzzles
with
Coins and Sticks

What can you do with circles and straight lines?
Or coins and sticks?
— Play games,
— solve puzzles,
— *and* have a lot of fun with them.

Some SEE-ZERS are jokes and practically
magical tricks. You will think so too when you
discover the fun of SEE-ZERS.

You have to *see* SEE-ZERS, *solve* SEE-
ZERS, and *play* with SEE-ZERS. You will find
the solutions, or answers, to the puzzles at the
back of the book.

SEE-ZERS

GAMES AND PUZZLES
WITH
COINS AND STICKS

by Gyles Brandreth
Pictures by Myron M. Morris

NUTMEG PRESS

Contents

© Text Gyles Brandreth 1976
© Illustrations Transworld Publishers 1976
© Revised edition Shelley Graphics Ltd. 1979
Original edition published in Great Britain under the title of
  Games and Puzzles with Coins and Matches
  by Transworld Publishers 1976
Published in the United States by Nutmeg Press
  a Division of Shelley Graphics Ltd. 1979
Printed in Canada

ISBN 0-89943-009-0

About Coins & Sticks

Coins of all shapes and sizes — round ones, square ones, and ones with holes in the middle — have been around and in everyday use for thousands of years. Coins have always been handy for buying things, and for a long time that's the only thing that people ever did with them. Then about a hundred years ago, someone realized that the little pieces of metal had a more entertaining use. You could invent and play hundreds of games and puzzles with them. The idea caught on in a big way, and soon just about everyone was playing coin games.

People loved the coin games so much in fact, that they started playing other games — this time with bits of wood. In those days the games were called "matchstick" games because people played them with big wooden matches.

Stick games are just as much fun today as they were when they were invented, but people no longer use matches, and only matches, to play them. Modern stick game fans use toothpicks, which are a lot safer, a lot cheaper, and easy to use. As a matter of fact, anything straight will do for stick games. Just think of what you could use — sticks, pencils, even pretzels! Only you must have lots of them, and they must be all of the same size. So, since toothpicks are just about your best choice, walk on over to the nearest supermarket and buy yourself a box of wooden or plastic toothpicks. For the little you spend on them, you will have hours and hours of brain-teasing fun.

GAMES WITH COINS

Fun For All

Most of the time, the best coin games are the ones that you can play on your own. So, you will find that nearly all the games and puzzles and challenges in this book allow you, and you alone, to pit your wits against a handful of small change, or a pile of toothpicks. There are games for two or more, of course, and we begin with one of the oldest and most popular of them.

This is a game for any number of players, so it's great for parties, or when you are with several friends. You begin by putting about twenty or thirty pennies on a tray in any arrangement you like — in the shape of a circle, or a square, or a cross, or scattered about — and you cover up the coins with a cloth. You then take the tray to the players, remove the cloth, and everybody gets five seconds to look at the coins. After you replace the cloth, the players guess how many coins are on the tray. You repeat this ten times, changing the number of coins on the tray each time, and the player who guesses the right number most often is the winner — and gets to keep the coins as a prize!

Only Two Can Play

Although it isn't quite as old and isn't nearly as simple, this game is another favorite. You need two players and fifty coins. Pennies will do nicely.

Lay out the fifty coins on the table in ten small piles, with five coins in each pile. Players move one at a time, and when it's his or her turn, a player can pick any pile of coins and take all the coins from that pile, or as many as he or she chooses. The player must take at least one coin at every turn and in each move can only take a coin, or coins, from one pile.

The loser is the player who is forced to pick up the last coin left on the table.

Star Turn

To take up the challenge of this game of coin patience, you must begin by drawing a large five-pointed star on a piece of paper. And, just in case you're not very good at drawing five-pointed stars, here's is one to give you the basic idea:

The aim of the game is to put your finger on one of the star's points, or on one of its *intersections* (where lines cross each other), pass over the next intersection and place a coin on the point or intersection beyond that. You must keep doing this until all the intersections and points of the star are covered with coins except one. If you succeed, you've won. If you don't, you've lost.

It sounds easy, which it is *if* you know the secret. And the secret is to start each time from a point or intersection which will allow you to fill up the point or intersection from which you started on your last move.

Once you've mastered the game, challenge your friends with it, but, unless you want them to succeed right away, don't give them the secret.

The Odds or Evens Trick

The trick: You are securely blindfolded and you invite a member of your audience — it may be the only member of your audience! — to place a pile of coins on the table in front of you. Without peeking and without touching the coins, you will now offer to add coins of your own to the pile on the table so that if the number is an even one you will make it an odd one, and if it is an odd one you will make it even. You do so. The audience is amazed.

The secret: You simply add an odd number of coins every time. It never fails.

Four Finger Exercise

Place a quarter on the tip of each finger of your right hand. Now try to work them all into a pile on the tip of your first finger. You can't use your thumb and, of course, you can't use your other hand. It isn't easy, but it can be done, so if you fail the first time, don't despair. Try, try, and try again.

10

Elbow Challenge

The elbow challenge is easy to explain, but tough to master. All you have to do is bend your arm backwards so that your knuckles are touching your shoulder and place a coin on your elbow. When the coin is in position, bring your hand down sharply and try to catch the coin before it reaches the ground.

When you've done it with one coin, try two. When two seems easy, try three. When three seems easy, try four. And keep going. The record is eighteen coins piled on one elbow!

Seven Up Challenge

Throw nine coins down onto the table. Remove four of them. Add three coins. And leave seven. Done it? Good. Now challenge a friend.

11

Not done it? Don't worry. You see, there's a trick to it. What you've got to do is add three coins to the four you removed from the original, or first nine coins. Once you've added the three new coins to the four you put aside, you will end up with seven! Easy, isn't it — once you know how.

PUZZLES WITH COINS

1 The Cross Challenge

Take six coins and arrange them on the table in the shape of a cross, like this:

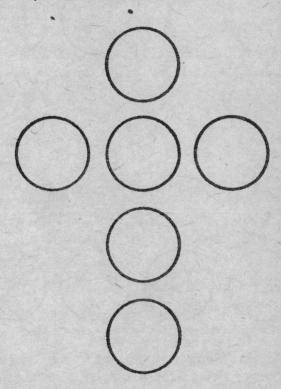

Now move just one of the coins and create two rows with four coins in each row.

2 The Square Challenge

Take twelve coins and arrange them on the table in the shape of a square, like this:

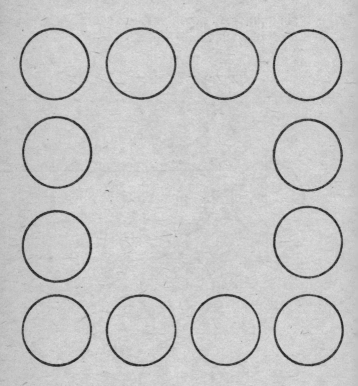

As you can see, there are four coins along each side of the square. Using the same twelve coins, form another square, but with the new square, see that you count five coins along each side.

3 Coins in a Circle

Take six coins and lay them out on the table in two colums like this:

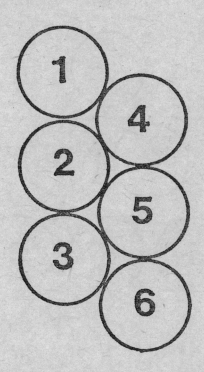

Now all you've got to do is make a circle of coins in just three moves! You can only move one coin at a time, and once you have moved it to its new position it must be touching at least two other coins.

4 Coins in a Pyramid

Take ten coins and lay them out on the table in the shape of a pyramid, like this:

Now move just three of the coins and turn the pyramid upside down.

5 The H Problem

Take seven coins and arrange them in a pattern to look like the letter H.

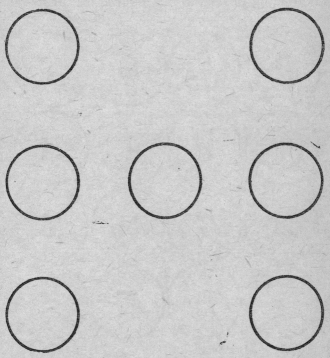

As you can see, counting the diagonal (slanting) lines as well as the vertical (up and down) and horizontal (straight across) lines, you have five rows with three coins in each row. Now add an extra two coins to the pattern and create a new pattern that makes ten rows with three coins in each row.

6 Sixteen Coins

Take sixteen coins and arrange them on the
table in four columns, with heads and tails
alternating, or next to each other, like this:

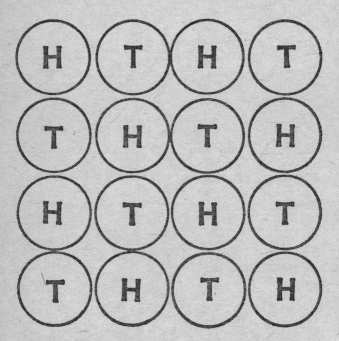

Now all you have got to do is rearrange the
coins so that the coins in each of the four vertical
columns are alike. In other words, you must end
up with one column of heads, one column of tails,
one column of heads, one column of tails. The
only problem is your hand is only allowed to
touch *two* of the sixteen coins!

7 Six in a Row

Find three nickels and three quarters and lay them out in a neat row, like this:

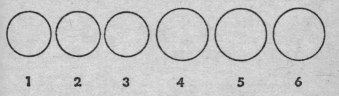

Now, in just three moves, moving two adjacent (next to each other) coins at a time, you have got to make a row of coins in which the nickels and quarters *alternate,* or change. There can't be any gaps between the coins!

8 Eight in a Row

Find four nickels and four quarters and lay them out in a row, like this:

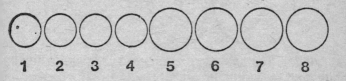

Now, in four moves, moving two adjacent (next to each other) coins at a time, you have got to make a row in which there are no gaps and the nickels and quarters alternate, or change.

9 The Fifth Coin

This puzzle, and the one on the next page, were invented by Henry Dudeney, an Englishman who lived in the last century. This genius with puzzles was a self-taught mathematician who loved brain teasers. Dudeney invented tens of thousands of mind-bending problems. These are two of his favorites.

Take four pennies and arrange them on the table, without using another coin or means of measurement, so that a *fifth* penny can be placed next to the four without moving them, as shown in the illustration. The shaded circle shows where the fifth penny should fit.

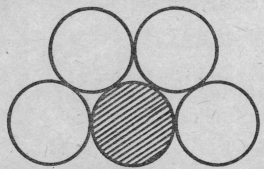

If you trust your eye alone you will probably fail to get the four in the correct position, but it can be done exactly and easily. How?

10 The Seventh Coin

Lay six pennies on the table and then arrange them as shown by the six white circles in the illustration, so that if a *seventh* penny — the shaded circle — were dropped in the center it would touch them all exactly.

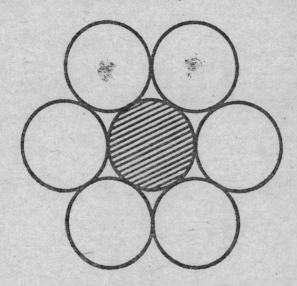

In this case, you are not allowed to lift any penny off the table — otherwise it would be no puzzle at all. And you can't measure or mark, either. So, get to it. You only need six pennies!

11 Head Over Heels

Take eight coins and lay them out in a circle, all heads up. They should look like this:

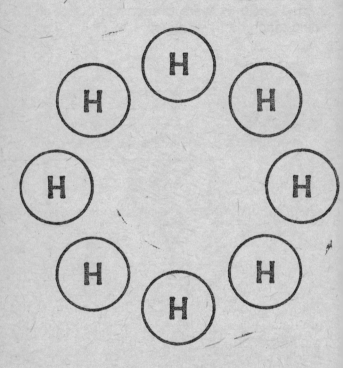

Starting from any coin you like, and moving clockwise or counter-clockwise, count one, two, three, four, and turn over the fourth coin so it's tails up. Start again from any coin that's heads up, repeating the whole thing. Keep at it until all the coins but one are tails up.

12 Nine-a-side

Take thirty-two coins and lay them out in a square so that there are nine coins on each side of the square.

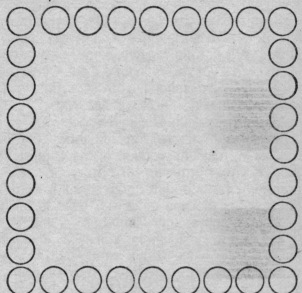

Now remove four coins and rearrange the remaining twenty-eight so that there are still nine coins on each side of the square.

Now remove an additional four coins and rearrange the remaining twenty-four so that there are still nine coins on each side of the square!

Finally, remove four more coins and rearrange the twenty that are left so that you can still count nine coins on each side of the square!

GAMES WITH STICKS

Nim

If you only happen to know one toothpick, or stick, game, the chances are that Nim's the one you know. Nim is the oldest and most famous of all the stick games for two, and if you haven't discovered it yet you're in for a treat. It is simple. It's exciting. It's satisfying. In fact, unless you happen to be *very* hard to please, Nim's a game that should keep you totally fascinated.

Of course, there are Nims and there are *Nims.* In other words, one version of the game is not always the same as another, and many arguments have begun because some Nim nut has insisted that his version of Nim is far, far better than some other Nim nut's version. Don't worry. All the best versions of Nim are in this book, so once you have read, marked, and learned these Nims you'll be ready to take on any Nim nut anytime, and anywhere.

If the dictionary is to be believed — and if you can't believe the dictionary, what *can* you believe? — Nim gets its name from an old verb "to nim" meaning "to take." Certainly, taking sticks is what the game of Nim is all about.

Begin by laying out fifteen toothpicks in three rows, like the layout of sticks on the following page. There should be seven toothpicks in the first row, five in the second, and three in the third.

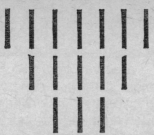

You and the other Nim player, your opponent, take turns and whenever it is your turn you pick up as many sticks as you like. However many or few they are though, they all have to come from the same row. The aim of the game is to force the other game player to pick up the last stick. Whoever has to pick up the last stick is the loser.

If you are a skillful player and have had a little practice you will discover that you don't ever need to lose! All you need to do is create one of two winning patterns and wait for your victory. In the first winning pattern you leave your opponent with just two rows of sticks with an equal number of sticks in each row.

For example, if it's your opponent's turn and the board looks like the diagram on this page, what can he or she do?

If your opponent takes all four sticks in one row, you take three from the other, leaving your

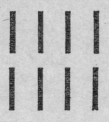

opponent the last stick. If your opponent takes three from one row, you take all four from the other, still leaving the last stick. If he or she takes two from one row, you take two from the other row, which means that you can beat your opponent on the next move. If he or she takes just one from one row, you take just one from the other row, and you will still triumph.

The other winning pattern to aim for looks like this:

If your opponent takes one stick from the top row, you must take one stick from the bottom row, leaving two rows of equal numbers. If your opponent takes one stick from the middle row, you must take two from the top. If your opponent takes both sticks in the middle, you must take all three from the top. If he or she takes two from the top, you must take one from the middle row. If your opponent takes all three from the top, you must take both sticks from the middle.

Of course, it sounds very complicated. It isn't. Once you've played a few games and seen the winning patterns in action, you'll be transformed into an unbeatable Nim master.

Nimble

Here's a game that comes from the great family of Nim. Some people call it the *real* version of the game. Others don't. At any rate, to play Nimble, you still need two players and fifteen sticks. The sticks must be laid out like this:

Players take turns to move, and a player can take one, two, or three sticks. The loser is the player who is forced to pick up the last stick.

If you want to win every time, all you have to do is to leave thirteen sticks first, then nine, and then five for your opponent to pick from. This way, you'll always be successful.

Nimbus

Nimbus is just like Nimble, except that you need a row of twenty-one sticks for this game.

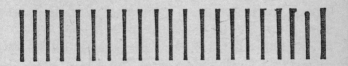

To be sure of winning here, all you need to do is always leave an uneven number of sticks for your opponent to pick from. It sounds like a very simple recipe for success, doesn't it? Well, try it and you will be pleasantly surprised to find that it works every time.

Niminy-Piminy

Here's yet another game from the Nim collection, this time calling for a row of twenty-five sticks:

Again, you need two players and each player takes a turn to pick up one, two, or three sticks. However, in this game it does not matter who picks up the last stick. What counts in Niminy-Piminy is *the number of sticks you end up with* after all the sticks have been picked up. If you end with an even number of sticks, you've won. If you end with an odd number of sticks, you've lost. Bad luck.

To be sure of winning, you've got to see that one of two situations happen: *either* your opponent has an even number of sticks in hand and there are twenty, seventeen, nine, or four sticks left in the row, *or*, your opponent has an odd number of sticks in hand and there are twenty-one, sixteen, thirteen, eight, or five sticks left in the row.

Nimcompoop

With this kind of Nim game you can really let yourself go. It is still a game for two players , but in it you are allowed to have any number of sticks you like — 10 or 10,000, and you can arrange them in any number of rows — 2 or 222. When it is his or her turn, a player can take any number of sticks from any one of the rows. A player cannot, however, take sticks from more than one row in any one turn. Once again, the player who picks up the last stick is the loser.

   If you want to be very daring and different, you can change the last rule and make the player who picks up the last stick of the last row of sticks the *winner*!

Kayles

Henry Dudeney, the great puzzler whose coin problems were on pages 20 and 21, invented this terrific stick game. It calls for two players and as many sticks as you like. If you use a thousand, the game will go on forever. If you use five, the game will be over in a flash. Twenty is about right. The sticks should be laid out on a table so that their ends are touching.

When their turns come up, players can take either one stick or two sticks, as long as the sticks are touching. For example, if there were three sticks left in the row and it was your turn,

1   **2**   **3**

you could take either sticks 1 and 2, or you could take sticks 2 and 3, or you could just take 1, or 2, or 3. Suppose you chose to take stick 2,

1   **3**

your unfortunate opponent would only be able to take either 1 or 3 — not both because they do not touch.

The winner is the player who picks up the last stick.

Matchboxes

In spite of its name, this game has got nothing to do with the little boxes that matches come in. The game gets its name from the way the table looks once you have set out your sticks to play.

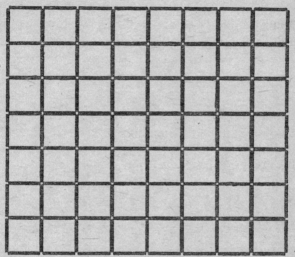

You can play with any number of sticks, but you must lay them out in a pattern of little squares so that they are all just barely touching.

The two players move in turn and, when a player's turn comes up, he or she can take either one stick or two sticks, as long as the sticks are touching. The two sticks do not have to be in a straight line. They can be at angles to one another, but they have to be touching.

The player who picks up the last stick is the winner.

Columns & Rows

Columns & Rows is very much like Matchboxes. It is a game for two, but it starts with a different layout. Naturally, the sticks must be set in rows and columns. The columns are the vertical (up and down) lines. The rows are the horizontal (straight across) ones. You can have any number you like.

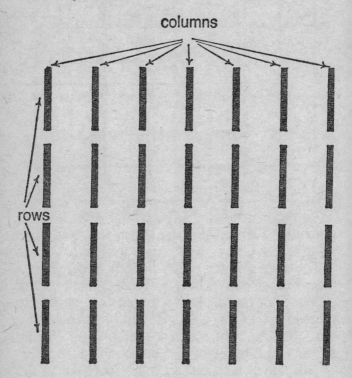

columns

rows

The players take turns to move, and each player can take any number of sticks from any one row or any one column. However, the sticks taken must be next to one another, with no gaps in between.

For example, if this is how the table looks after a few moves,

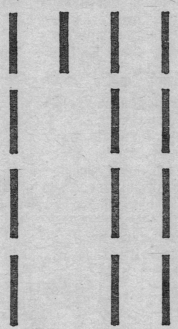

the next player can take either
the whole of the
first column,
or the one stick in the
second column,

or the whole of the
third column,
or the whole of the
fourth column,
or the whole of the
first row,
or the first stick or the
last two sticks
in the second row,
or the first stick or the
last two sticks
in the third row,
or the first stick or the
last two sticks
in the fourth row,
or any single,
individual stick.

What a player cannot do is to take the whole of the second, third, or fourth rows, because in each case there is a gap between the first stick in the row and the last two.

The winner is the player who picks up the last stick.

Maxey

A marvelous stick game maniac named Maxey Brooke invented this great game. It is different from all the other games — just as entertaining, but a bit more difficult.

You need two players, ten toothpicks, and a paper and pencil. Begin by drawing seven parallel lines on the piece of paper. Parallel lines are straight like railroad tracks, or Venetian blinds, and equally far apart. Each line should be roughly the length of a stick (toothpick) and the lines should all be a little less than a stick-length apart.

Each player has five sticks to play with and can play one stick at a time. The players take turns laying sticks along the drawn lines. If two sticks happen to be side by side, a player can place a stick across both of them.

Players score one point every time they play a stick parallel to a played stick, and two points every time they manage to play a stick across two played sticks.

The player with the most points wins.

All Square

When you play this game with paper and pencil it is usually called Boxes. When you play it with sticks, it's usually called All Square. The rules are simple.

There are two players and each player has 40 sticks. They take turns to play and can only play one stick at a time. Each played stick must touch either end of a stick already played, at an angle of either 90 degrees or 180 degrees:

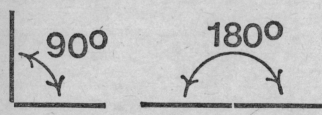

There can be no more than eight sticks in any one horizontal (straight across) or vertical (up and down) row. The player who plays a stick that completes a square scores a point for the square and gets another turn.

When all the sticks have been played, the player with the most points is the winner.

Spillikins

If Nim, and Nimble, and Nimbus, and Niminy-Piminy, and Nincompoop, and Kayles, and Matchboxes, and Columns & Rows, and Maxey, and All Square have left you exhausted and brain-drained, Spillikins is what you need. It isn't a high-powered game like the rest. It isn't difficult. It isn't demanding. It's just delicious.

To play Spillikins you need an egg cup, or a tiny, tiny cup, a box of toothpicks, and two or more players. Stand the toothpicks inside the egg cup, and let the players take turns to move.

The first player removes one stick from the egg cup and carefully lays it across the top of the other toothpicks in the egg cup. The second player does the same. So does the third. This goes on and on around the group, with players removing the toothpicks from the egg cup, one by one, and laying them across the remaining toothpicks. When all the toothpicks have been taken out of the egg cup and laid across the top, the game is over.

Of course, a player is going to be very, very lucky if, while removing a toothpick from the egg cup and laying it across the top, some of the other toothpicks aren't knocked over. Every toothpick a player knocks over during a move, must be collected and held.

At the end of the game, the player with the fewest toothpicks is the winner.

Stick-taker

Like Spillikins, this game isn't so much a battle of wits where only two can play; it's more of a light-hearted party game for the whole family. You can have any number of players, and each player must have three toothpicks. And, you will need a leader to play the part of the Stick-taker.

The Stick-taker begins by giving every one of the players a number. If, for example, there are four players, one of them will be Number One, one will be Number Two, and so on. When the players have their numbers, the Stick-taker tells a story. It can be any kind of story about anything, but the Stick-taker must bring the numbers of the players into the story. Just after the Stick-taker mentions a number, he or she taps the table with a hand. Now, if the Stick-taker taps the table before the player whose number was mentioned manages to tap the table, the Stick-taker takes one of that player's sticks as a penalty. However, if the player whose number was mentioned is able to tap the table before the Stick-taker, he or she holds on to all of the sticks. And, any player who taps the table by mistake must give one stick to the Stick-taker.

The game goes on until all the players have lost their sticks to the Stick-taker, and then it becomes someone else's turn to be the Stick-taker and tell the tale.

Last stick

Last Stick is another game that's good to play at parties. You can have as many players as you like, and as many sticks, but just so the game does not go on all day and night, figure on about 10 sticks per player.

Begin by putting all the sticks in a pile in the middle of the table. Then choose a number between 1 and 10. That number will be the largest number of sticks that a player can take in any one move. When the number has been chosen, you can start the game. As usual, players take turns. Each player takes one or more sticks, but must take at least one and no more than the maximum allowed.

The player who is forced to pick up the last stick is the loser.

Roman Challenge

Hand your opponent six sticks and ask him or ask her to lay them out on a table so that they make three and a half-dozen. Your opponent will look puzzled, will try, and then fail. Then, you can take the six sticks and lay them out like this:

In Roman numerals, III means three and VI means six, so that with six sticks you have managed to make three and a half-dozen!

PUZZLES WITH STICKS

1 The Twelve Stick Challenge

For each of the seven puzzles on this page you must begin with an arrangement of twelve toothpicks that looks like this:

a. Now, move two sticks and make seven squares.
b. Move three sticks and leave three squares.
c. Move four sticks and leave three squares.
d. Move four sticks and make ten squares.
e. *Remove* one stick, move four others and make eleven squares.
f. *Remove* two sticks and leave two squares.
g. *Remove* three sticks, move two others and leave three squares.

2 The Twenty-four Stick Challenge

For each of the six puzzles on this page, you must begin with an arrangement of twenty-four toothpicks that looks like this:

a. Remove four sticks and leave five squares.
b. Remove six sticks and leave three squares.
c. Remove six sticks and leave five squares.
d. Remove eight sticks and leave two squares.
e. Remove eight sticks and leave three squares.
f. Remove eight sticks and leave four squares.

3 Two Dozen Sticks

For each of the nine puzzles on this page you will need two dozen toothpicks.

a. With twenty-four sticks make four squares.
b. With twenty-four sticks make five squares.
c. With twenty-four sticks make six squares.
d. With twenty-four sticks make seven squares.
e. With twenty-four sticks make eight squares.
f. With twenty-four sticks make fourteen squares
g. With twenty-four sticks make twenty squares.
h. With twenty-four sticks make forty-two squares.
i. With twenty-four sticks make one hundred and ten squares!

4 The Farmer's Children

Farmer Jones, whose handsome cows are famous all over Ohio, lives in a beautiful farmhouse in the middle of an enormous field.

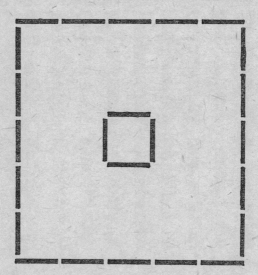

Farmer Jones has six sons and he wants to leave his land to them. How can he divide the land up equally between the six? (The sons aren't going to get a share of the house, by the way. That is being left to Mrs. Jones.)

Farmer Jones also has two sons who want to leave the farm, and Mrs. Jones feels that they should share the land too. If Mrs. Jones gets her way and Farmer Jones decides to leave his land (apart from the house) to all eight children, how could he divide it equally between the eight?

5 Josh's Boys

Farmer Josh, the best-known pig breeder in Iowa, has the same sort of problem as his distant relative, Farmer Jones. It's not quite as bad as in Farmer Jone's case, though, because he has only five boys.

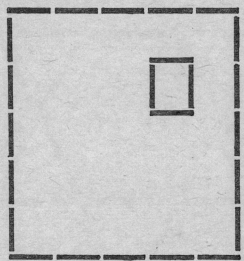

What Farmer Josh wants to leave to his five sons is his large field. He doesn't want to leave them the feeding trough that's in it, because none of them are interested in pig-breeding. Instead, he is saving this piece of land for a park, or nature area.

The question is how can Farmer Josh divide his land (except for the feeding trough) equally among his children?

6 Terrific Triangles

Make this star-shaped pattern with eighteen toothpicks:

Now move two of the toothpicks, and make the number of triangles in the pattern fewer by two. There should be six triangles, not eight.

7 Squarely Triangular

With eight toothpicks, make two squares and four triangles.

8 Terrifying Triangles

Make this unusual pattern with thirteen toothpicks:

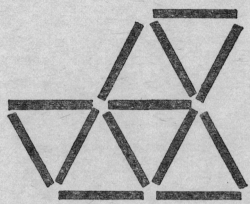

Now take away just three toothpicks and leave
three triangles.

9 Triangular

Take nine toothpicks and arrange them like this:

Now move three of the toothpicks and make
five triangles.

10 All Fours

Take sixteen toothpicks and form this pattern with them:

Now take away four toothpicks and leave four triangles.

11 Small Squares

Take eight toothpicks and form this pattern with them:

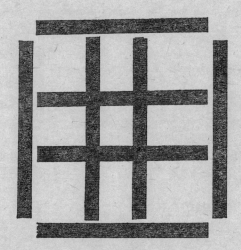

Now take away two toothpicks and leave three squares.

12 Six out of Nine

Make six squares with nine toothpicks.

13 Three out of Five

Take fifteen toothpicks and arrange them like this:

Now take away three of them and leave three squares.

14 Three out of Six

Take a dozen toothpicks and arrange them like this:

There are six equilateral triangles in that pattern. Equilateral triangles have sides of the same length. Move just four of the toothpicks and leave a pattern of three equilateral triangles.

15 Sane Sum

Now you're going to meet a lot of complicated Roman numerals. Before you get to them, try to solve a much simpler sum using everyday figures. Simply arrange five toothpicks in a sum that totals fourteen! And then use another four toothpicks to write the figure fourteen.

16 Roman Puzzles

For the next six problems you face, you need to know your Roman numerals. Just in case they have slipped your memory, here they are again, from 1 to 30:

1 = I	16 = XVI
2 = II	17 = XVII
3 = III	18 = XVIII
4 = IV	19 = XIX
5 = V	20 = XX
6 = VI	21 = XXI
7 = VII	22 = XXII
8 = VIII	23 = XXIII
9 = IX	24 = XXIV
10 = X	25 = XXV
11 = XI	26 = XXVI
12 = XII	27 = XXVII
13 = XIII	28 = XXVIII
14 = XIV	29 = XXIX
15 = XV	30 = XXX

a Move just one toothpick, to make this simple sum work out:

$$III - II = IV$$

b Move just one toothpick and make this simple sum work out:

$$IV - II = V$$

c This sum is not quite as simple, but you still only need to move one toothpick to make it work out. In fact, you may be able to work out two answers to the same problem.

$$VI - IV = IX$$

d To make this sum work out, you must move two toothpicks. Try.

e For this Roman sum, you must *remove* three toothpicks and nudge one to make it work out correctly.

f And for this, the last of our Roman teasers, you don't need to touch a single toothpick to make the sum work out correctly. So what should you do instead?

17 Climbing Frame

With thirty-six toothpicks make a pattern of
thirteen squares that look like this:

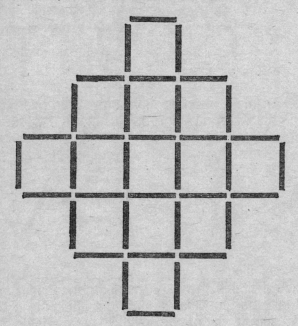

Now take away four of the toothpicks and
leave nine squares.

18 Touch and Go

Take six toothpicks and arrange them on the
table so that each toothpick is touching the other
five.

19 The Six Containers

With thirteen toothpicks you can form a pattern that features six equal-sized containers. It will look like this:

Suppose you only have twelve toothpicks, but you still want six equal-sized containers. How do you do it?

20 All Square

Take sixteen toothpicks and use them to form this pattern:

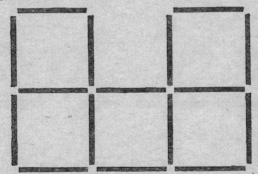

Now remove three toothpicks and create four *equal* squares.

21 Long Division

Take sixteen toothpicks and form a figure that looks like this:

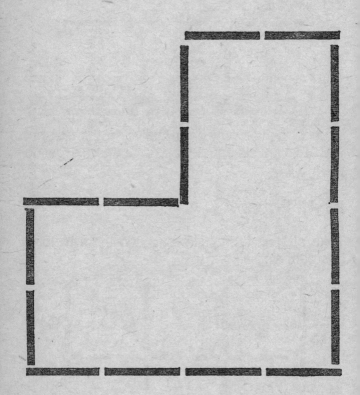

Now add eight more toothpicks and, in doing so, *divide* the figure into four parts of equal size and shape.

22 Amazing

With thirty-five toothpicks form this shape on the table:

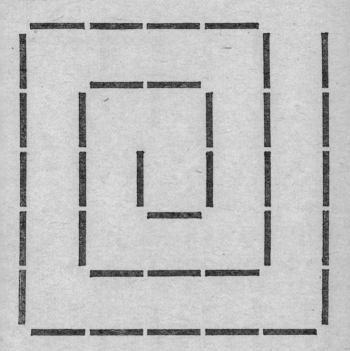

Now move four toothpicks and make three squares.

23 Eleven

With fifteen toothpicks make eleven squares.

24 Ten

Here are four toothpicks:

Add five more and make ten!

25 Nine

Here are six toothpicks:

Add five more and make nine!!

26 All You Need

With sixteen toothpicks make four squares, like this:

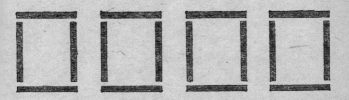

Now take away four of the toothpicks, move three of the remaining ones, and see if you can end up with whatever it is that makes the world go round.

27 Goodbye

Finally, lay out eight toothpicks like this:

Add eleven more and you will find yourself at the end.

SOLUTIONS TO COIN PUZZLES

1 Cross Challenge

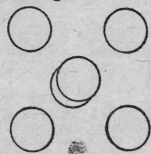

There are two coins in the middle.

2 Square Challenge

There are two coins at each corner.

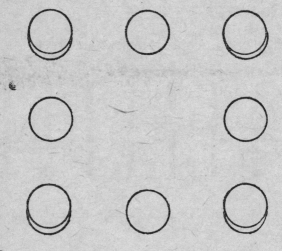

3 Coins in a Circle

Here are your three moves:

1. Move 4 to touch 5 and 6.
2. Move 5 to touch 1 and 2.
3. Move 1 to touch 5 and 4.

The circle should now look like this:

4 Coins in a Pyramid

Here are your three moves:

1. Move 1 to bottom row and place it between and under 8 and 9.
2. Move 7 up two rows and place it to the left of 2.
3. Move 10 up two rows and place it to the right of 3.

5 The H Problem

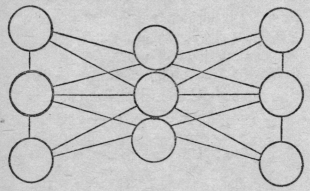

6 Sixteen Coins

Put your first and second fingers on the two asterisked coins and bring them around into the positions shown by the dotted lines:

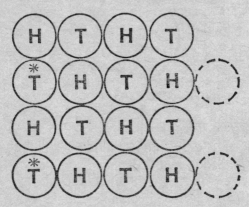

Now, with your fingers still on the same two coins, push the six coins (the three coins in the second row and the three coins in the bottom row) to the left, and you will end up with the columns looking just as you want them:

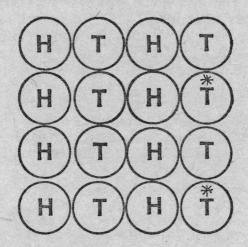

7 Six in a Row

Here are your three moves:
1. Move coins 1 and 2 to the right of 6.
2. Move coins 6 and 1 to the right of 2.
3. Move coins 3 and 4 to the right of 5.

8 Eight in a Row

Here are your four moves:
1. Move coins 6 and 7 to the left of 1.
2. Move coins 3 and 4 to the right of 5.
3. Move coins 7 and 1 to the right of 2.
4. Move coins 4 and 8 to the right of 6.

9 The Fifth Coin

Here, in his own words, is the solution to Henry Dudeney's puzzle:

"First place the four pennies together as in the first diagram; then remove number 1 to the new position shown in the second diagram; and finally, carefully withdraw number 4 downward, move it to the left and upward and place it between 2 and 3. Then the coins will be in the positions shown in the third diagram and the fifth penny may be added so that it will exactly touch all four."

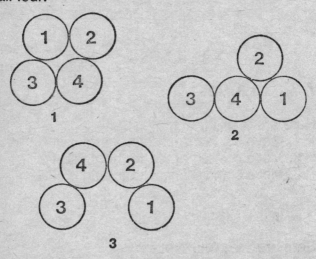

A glance at the last diagram will show how difficult it is to judge by eye alone the correct distance from number 1 to number 3. You are almost certain to place them too near together.

10 The Seventh Coin

First arrange the pennies as in the first diagram.

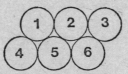

Then carefully shift 6 into the position shown in the second diagram.

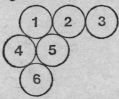

Next place 5 against 2 and 3 to get the position in the third diagram. Number 3 can now be placed in the position indicated by the dotted circle in the diagram, and a seventh penny dropped into the center to fit exactly.

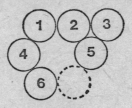

11 Head over Heels

Always count in the same direction, leaving out one coin each time before starting the next count.

12 Nine-a-side

Here are twenty-eight coins in a square, with nine coins on each side. At each of the four corners to the square there are two coins, and in the center of each of the four sides there are five coins.

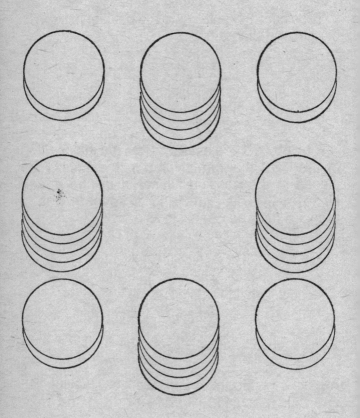

Here are twenty-four coins in a square, with nine coins on each side. The square is made up of eight piles of coins, with three coins in each pile.

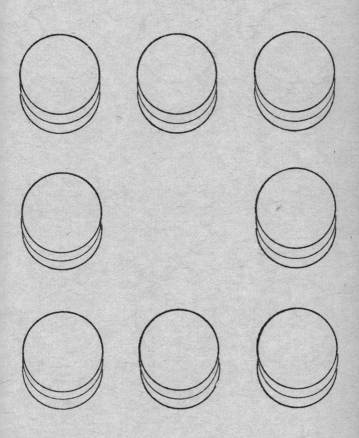

Here are twenty coins in a square, with nine coins on each side. At each of the four corners of the square there are four coins, and in the center of each of the four sides there is one coin.

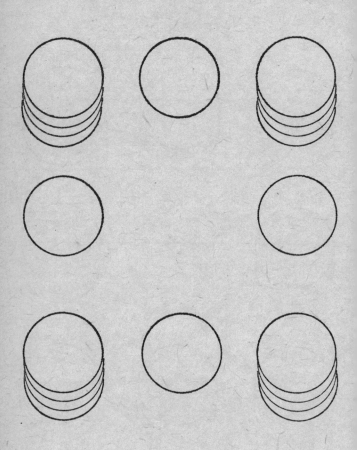

SOLUTIONS
TO STICK PUZZLES

1 The Twelve Stick Challenge

a.

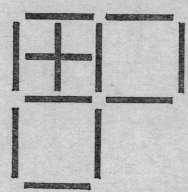

b.

c.

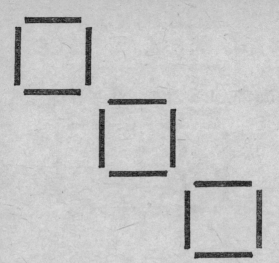

d.

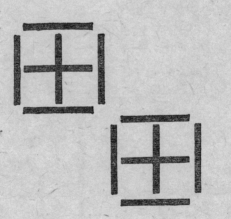

e.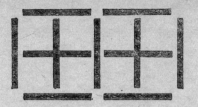

f.

g.

a.

or

b.

c.

d.

or

e.

f.

or

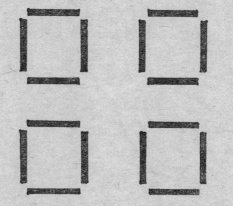

3 Two Dozen Sticks

a.

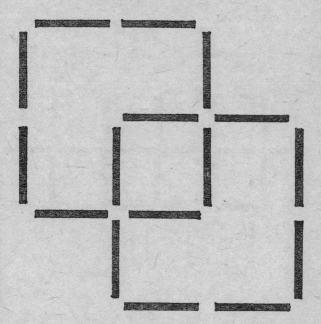

b.

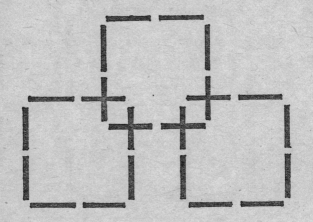

c.

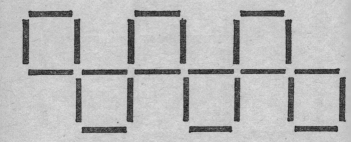

d.

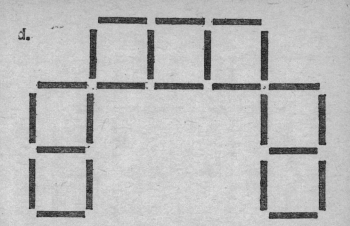

e.

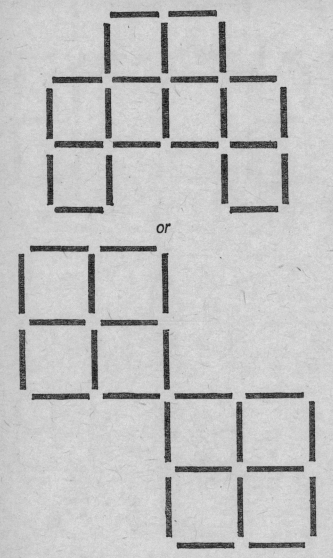

or

f.

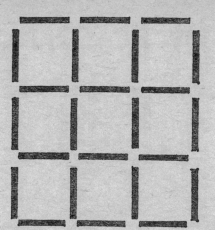

g.

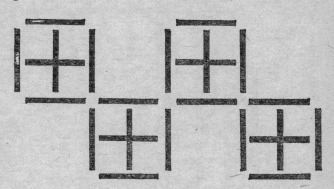

h.

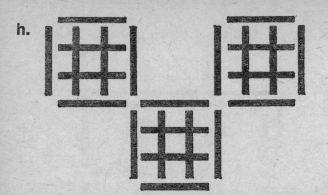

i.

4 The Farmer's Children

With the land divided equally between six:

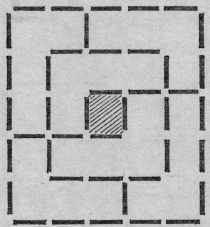

And the land divided equally between eight:

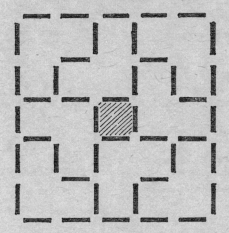

5 Josh's Boys

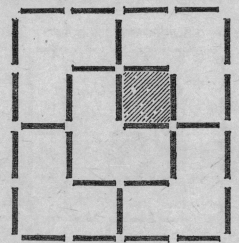

6 Terrific Triangles

7 Squarely Triangular

8 Terrifying Triangles

9 Triangular

11 Small Squares

12 Six out of Nine

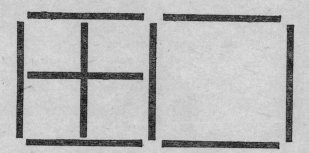

13 Three out of Five

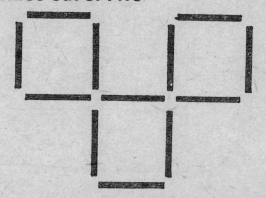

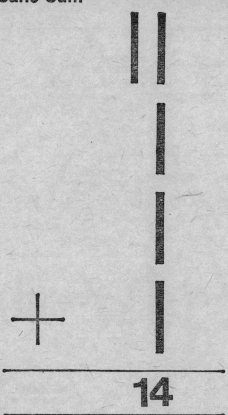

$$14 = 14$$

a.

III + II = V

b. IV + I = V

c. V + IV = IX

or

VI + IV = X

d. VII − V = II

e.

f. All you need to do is walk around to the other side of the table and the sum makes sense!

17 The Climbing Frame

18 Touch and Go

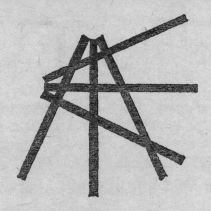

19 The Six Containers

20 All Square

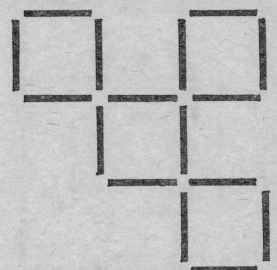

21 Long Division

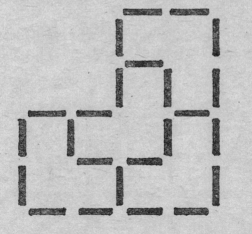

22 Amazing

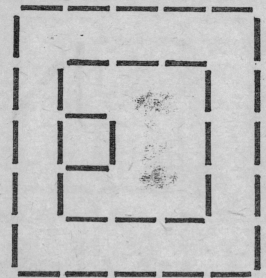

23 Eleven

There are eight small squares and three big squares. Don't forget the square in the middle!

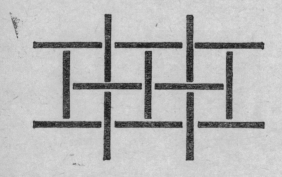

24 Ten

TEN

25 Nine

NINE

26 All You Need

LOVE

THE
END